Mind Over Mutter:

160 Practical Tips
for Giving
Great Presentations

by Barry F. Mitsch

Mind Over Mutter: 160 Practical Tips for Giving Great Presentations

Special thanks to Monica Loewy Caplan for formatting the text and editing, Wendy Coulter for the cover design, Jim Lied of MicroPress for administrative support, and Marcia Reynolds for contributing her creative energy for the book title. And thanks to the hundreds of professionals who have directly or indirectly contributed ideas for this book.

Additional copies can be ordered from www.pyramidresource.com. Volume discounts are available.

Dedication

To DJ, Jessica, and Hank.

Contents

Introduction

I entered graduate school at the University of North Carolina in 1981 following a two-year stint in the Peace Corps. A requirement for a Master's Degree in Environmental Sciences was a public defense of my master's research. I dreaded this event from the very day I learned of its necessity for graduation. Did I really want the degree that badly? Wouldn't it be easier just to get a job? I was faced with the decision of dropping out of school or facing my fear. Twenty years later, I still have the fear but have learned many skills and strategies that can benefit any professional who needs to give presentations as part of their work or civic life.

Facing my fear led to a local Toastmasters Club in Chapel Hill. Toastmasters was the starting point on my learning curve and I recommend that organization to anyone looking for immediate and consistent help with public speaking. The skills I learned in Toast-

Mind Over Mutter:
160 Practical Tips for Giving Great Presentations

masters led to the successful completion of my Master's Degree and also contributed to my being hired by a technical services company after graduation. I got the job not because of a superior resume, but because of a superior presentation that I gave to the company during the interview process.

The benefits of being a proficient speaker were obvious. As I entered the work force, I noticed there were many people who hated giving presentations. And even when they spoke, they were less than inspiring and often very ineffective. There was a dire need for a practical approach to developing and delivering effective presentations.

Eventually my burgeoning interest in this topic led to the development of a workshop I called "Technically Speaking." The workshop created many speaking opportunities, production of a video-based companion program, involvement in distance learning using satellite and video-conferencing technology, and the opportunity to work with hundreds of professionals in group and private sessions.

I have accumulated an immense amount of practical knowledge about giving presentations and wanted to create a way to share that with as many people as possible. I also wanted to create a means for learning even more about this essential skill from people working in diverse fields around the globe. So my hope is that this little book will be a valuable resource for professionals who deliver presentations in all arenas of business and civic life, and that people will share their practical tips for inclusion in later editions.

Barry F. Mitsch
Cary, North Carolina

Getting Started

Getting Started

1   There are no rules

In my opinion, the only rule that applies to presentation skills—and public speaking—is that "there are no rules." Everyone has different strengths and weaknesses, and some people can get away with things others should never attempt. The key is to optimize your individual talents. Use your God-given ability to its highest level. Find out what works for you and what doesn't. Constantly observe other speakers and try to adopt styles and techniques that fit your personality.

Getting Started

2 **The critical first step**

A successful presentation must have a clearly defined purpose or objective. There are essentially two types of objectives. An informative objective focuses on what you want people to KNOW; a persuasive objective focuses on what you want people to DO. Before you begin to develop content for a presentation, define a clear objective.

3 **Crafting an objective**

The easiest way to develop an objective for a presentation is to answer one or both of these questions: 1) Why am I giving this presentation? 2) What do I want to have happen as a result of the presentation?

Getting Started

4   Measure the outcome

The best objectives are those that can be measured with an outcome. How many people signed up for my offering? How many people followed the procedure I discussed? Was my proposal accepted? You will have a more concise objective when you can tie it to an outcome.

5   The critical second step

The purpose of any presentation is to meet the needs of an audience—it's not about the speaker! Once you have a clear objective, you must analyze the audience in terms of as many factors as possible—knowledge, receptivity to your topic, experience, authority, decision-making power, influence, age, sex, context of your presentation with others, and much more.

Getting Started

6   Customizing a business presentation

Talk to colleagues who have presented to this client in the past and ask them what worked and what did not work. Ask about the conference room or meeting location and understand any logistical challenges. Do a dry run for a small group of colleagues and ask for input and suggestions for improvement.

7   Use the Internet

Use the internet to research corporate information prior to any presentation to a new client and/or company. Every company has a web-site that usually includes press releases and current information that will be useful in customization. Ask permission to use their logo to customize any slides or handout material.

Getting Started

8   Customizing for a conference presentation

Become best friends with the conference planner.
Request a list of attendees and contact 3-4 of them
personally to discuss their needs and expectations. Get
the name of the audio-visual technician who is coordi-
nating the conference and become their best friend as
well. Request a sketch of the room where you will be
speaking.

9   More on conference presentations

Get the agenda and note the persons and topics who
will be speaking before and after you. Contact other
speakers on the agenda and ask them if they can share
any information they may have to help you customize.

Getting Started

10   Create a target plan

A target plan consists of a clearly defined purpose or objective for the presentation, coupled with an analysis of the listeners to whom you will be presenting. When you have that information clearly defined, choosing content for the presentation simply requires that you answer the question, "What content do I need to include in the presentation to meet *this* objective for *this* group of people?"

Getting Started

11   Getting people to listen

Most people are not great listeners; they simply have
too much on their personal agendas. The best presentations overcome listening limitations by being well
organized, customized, and include many "change
elements" that keep people's attention. A change
element can be visual or vocal, high-tech or low-tech—
just something that keeps the content more interesting.

12   Prepare an introduction

If you are going to be introduced, it is best to prepare
your own introduction. The introduction should
answer the questions: Why this speaker? Why this
subject? Why this audience? Only include information that will enhance the subject of your presentation and establish your credibility for this specific
subject being presented to this specific audience.

Getting Started

13 A great resource

Epson sponsors a comprehensive web site that is great for helping you with all phases of presenting. Visit www.presentersonline.com.

Notes:

Mind Over Mutter:
160 Practical Tips for Giving Great Presentations

Formulating Content

Formulating Content

14   Organization

The oldest theories about presentations go back to the days of Aristotle. His three keys to a successful presentation are the logos, pathos, and ethos. The logos is how you organize your thoughts...it must have a logical order. Consider organizing your main points in a way that makes the most sense to your listeners.

15   The "three pointer"

The best presentations have limited numbers of key points. Try to use the old "three pointer" to organize your content. First, next, last—past, present, future—problem, cause, solution. Keep the content in bite-size chunks and people will find it easier to follow and remember.

Formulating Content

16   Tell 'em, tell 'em, told 'em

The oldest and simplest advice about organizing a presentation is to "tell 'em what you're gonna tell 'em (the opening), tell 'em (the body), and tell 'em what you told 'em (the closing). It works all the time.

17   Limited numbers of key points

While the old three-pointer is great, complex pre-sentations often require more than three main points. But never exceed 7...it's just too much information for an audience to digest, regardless of the length of your talk. Bundle, categorize, combine your content into themes and "chunks"...get it covered in no more than 7 main topic areas or main points.

Formulating Content

18   **Brainstorm the content**

The easiest way to develop a presentation quickly is to brainstorm everything you know about your topic. Start with a blank sheet of paper and fill it up with ideas. Then simply select content to meet your objective for a specific audience.

19   **Verbal before visual**

Many speakers begin crafting a presentation by first developing their visual aids. Avoid this tendency and work on the verbal content first. Then, your visuals will more likely be appropriate and have more impact.

Formulating Content

20   Story telling

Personal stories always add power to a presentation if they relate to your purpose. Always look for "real-life" examples that help you emphasize your points and add credibility to your presentation.

21   Beware of technical jargon

Jargon and acronyms can spoil a good presentation. Unless you are 100% certain that everyone in your audience can speak your "language," get rid of any unfamiliar technical terms and be sure to define any acronym at least once before you use it.

Ideas?

Mind Over Mutter:
160 Practical Tips for Giving Great Presentations

Practice Techniques

Practice Techniques

22   Practicing

You can improve your presentation if you have time to practice it with a small group and get some feedback. In lieu of practicing with a live audience, focus on private vocal practice where you can walk through the entire presentation.

23   Practice with your last set of visual aids and notes

Always have a practice session that includes the final draft of any visual material and the last draft of any notes you will be using. This will help familiarize yourself with the tools that will be critical to your success.

Practice Techniques

24   Practice and don't stop

Once you feel you are ready to go, have a practice
session where you do not allow yourself to stop once
you have begun the presentation. Chances are you may
get lost or forget a small part of your presentation, and
that's perfectly fine. Just don't stop, feel what its like to
get lost and recover during practice and you will be
more confident during the real thing.

Practice Techniques

25 Videotaping

Videotaping a practice presentation is one of the most powerful tools to improve your presentation style. Just about everybody owns a camcorder, use it to help you become a better speaker.

26 Fast forward advantage

One of the most powerful observational tools is to watch yourself on videotape in the "fast forward" mode. Fast forward will highlight any repetitive movements, nervous habits and distracting mannerisms that can be minimized.

Practice Techniques

27   Toastmasters

The best place to practice your presentation skills on an ongoing basis is at a Toastmasters Club. Check www.toastmasters.org for a club in your area.

Practice Techniques

28   Look for places to practice

The best way to become a better presenter is to give more presentations. If your work does not give you frequent opportunities, get involved in some extracurricular activities that do. Join a Toastmasters Club, become an officer in a civic club, teach a class at church or a community college, volunteer to read at a school...the possibilities are endless. The better speakers are better because they have more opportunities.

Practice Techniques

29   Get a buddy...or two

Presenters get better by giving more presentations...and getting constructive feedback after each presentation to find out how they can improve. How can you get this feedback? A great way is to have your work team attend a presentation skills workshop together. Agree to provide each other feedback on style and content after each future presentation.

Notes:

Mind Over Mutter:
160 Practical Tips for Giving Great Presentations

Openings

Openings

30 A standard opening

A fool-proof opening has three parts: 1) provide some brief background information that serves to put everyone on common ground; 2) state the objective or purpose of your presentation; and 3) preview your main points.

31 The value of previewing main points

By previewing your main points, you help to establish a pattern for listeners to follow. When you tell them you will talk about points A, B, and C, they figuratively label file folders in their minds with points A, B, and C. As you move from point to point in your presentation, the preview of the main points helps them follow you with closer attention.

Openings

32 Humor

Many speakers begin a presentation with some humor. Humor is only effective if it relates to the content and objective of your presentation. Avoid using humor if it is not relevant to your content.

33 Personal Stories

A personal story often makes a great opening, especially if it relates to the critical content of your presentation. Keep stories short, concise, and relative.

Openings

34   Quotes

A relevant quotation from a famous person can grab
attention. There are many sites on the world-wide web
where you can search for great quotations. Enter "quotations" at www.google.com and you will find a plethora
of resources.

Closings

Closings

35 The essential closing element

Always summarize your main points in your closing. This is where you tell them what you told them. Many speakers commonly overlook this essential element.

36 Don't end on a question

Many speakers end their presentations by asking for questions. If you do have a question and answer period, always reserve the last few minutes for yourself to close again by summarizing your main points. Get the last word, it's your presentation!

Transitions

Transitions

37   Verbal Transitions

You can help your audience follow your presentation by providing clear verbal transitions between the elements of your talk. Transitions serve as the bridges that connect your opening, main points and closing.

38   Transitions from opening to body

Try these simple transitions: 1) "Let's get started...the first point I want to make is..." 2)"First, let's establish the reasons for the [problem, overrun, etc.]" 3) "My first main point is..." 4) [display a visual aid] "Let's take a look at..."

Transitions

39   Transitions from main point to main point

Try these transitions between main points: 1) "That gives you the big picture; now let's focus on some details." 2) "Now that I have outlined the features of the product, let's talk about the benefits." 3) "Those are the pros and cons of alternative A, now let's talk about alternative B."

40   Putting on the brakes

Transitions from the body of your talk to the conclusion are often referred to as "brake lights." Examples include: 1) "...in conclusion..." 2) "Let me summarize...: 3) "Let's pull it all together..." Use a brake light to indicate you have completed the main body of your presentation.

Ideas?

Mind Over Mutter:
160 Practical Tips for Giving Great Presentations

Vocal Skills

Vocal Skills

41 Tape record your voice

One of the best ways to improve your vocal skills is to record yourself while speaking in any situation. Purchase a small, hand-held tape recorder and take it with you to every speaking engagement. Listen to yourself and ask how you can improve your vocal delivery with subtle changes in pace, pitch, and volume.

42 Green eggs and ham

A great place to practice vocal variety is to read children's books aloud to kids. Some of the same speech alterations you use to make a children's book interesting to kids can be used in a business presentation.

Vocal Skills

43 Better too fast than too slow

It's better to speak too fast than too slow, people can process information at a very rapid rate. However, nothing beats selective changes in pace to emphasize keys points and maintain interest.

44 Better too loud than too soft

Your audience must be able to hear you. But, you can make great use of changes in volume to emphasize key points, provide passion, exude enthusiasm, and add polish to your delivery.

Vocal Skills

45 Pausing is good

Researchers actually found that people remember what is said after a pause. It helps draw attention and can be used for emphasis and drama. Don't be afraid to pause on occasion to collect your thoughts and stay on track. This can also be important before answering a question. Give yourself a few seconds to formulate a response.

46 Minimize the ah's

Most people do not realize how often they use non-words such as "ah" or "um" until they are video or audio taped. The first step in minimizing these distracters is to be aware of their presence in your speech pattern. Invest in a hand-held tape recorder and record your presentations. Be aware of the "ahs" and work to minimize their presence.

Vocal Skills

47   Amplification

You will typically need a microphone for audiences greater than 40 people. But this is not always the case since it depends on the quality of the room and the acoustics. Determine if you will need amplification by doing a dry run with colleagues seated at the rear of the room to give you feedback on how well they can hear you.

48   The power of the voice

Remember that most of the greatest speeches of the 20th century were only heard by most people, not seen. From Churchill to King, the great speeches are remembered because of their vocal quality, not because of superior visuals aids or body language. Work on improving your vocal power and your presentations will improve dramatically.

Notes:

Mind Over Mutter:
160 Practical Tips for Giving Great Presentations

Using Technology

Using Technology

49   You are the best visual aid

With all the technology available for presentations, remember that YOU are still the focus of the presentation. Technology is a TOOL, not the driving force of a great presentation.

50   Keep the lights on

Your presentation will be more powerful in a lighted room. Choose technology that allows you to present without turning off lights. The newer projectors are very bright and can be used in well-lit rooms.

Using Technology

51   Overhead projectors

This is a piece of equipment that is tried but true and still a useful tool in the computer age. If you use an overhead, place your transparencies in FlipFrames™ available from 3M Company. These frames make your transparencies easy to transport, they will appear more professional on the screen, and you can use the white space on the flip sheets for notes. Just practice the "flipping" action before your presentation.

52   The latest technology

One of the best sources of information on presentation technology is www.presentations.com. This is a great web site and they also publish a very useful magazine.

Using Technology

53   Slide projectors

This is another "ancient" tool that still has some usage. Many rooms have rear-projection set-ups, be sure you test your slides after you load them to make sure they account for front or rear projection.

54   Advancing slides with a computer

There are many ways to advance slides using a computer. You can advance slides using the space bar, the page-up command, with a mouse click, or even with the roller function on the mouse. Practice using all these approaches and use the method you find most comfortable.

Using Technology

55   **Number your slides**

Even when using a computer, it's good to number your slides. Someone may want you to refer back to a specific slide. In most presentation software packages, you can get to the slide quickly by tapping on the number key for the slide and hitting the return key. If you need to get to slide #7...tap on 7 then return and you are there.

56   **Use a "bumper" slide**

A common occurrence in a computer presentation is advancing past the last slide and having the desktop appear on the screen. This looks sloppy and can be avoided by inserting a bumper slide. This is a final slide that serves as a bookmark for the speaker. It can be a corporate logo, a repeat of a title slide, or simply a blank background slide.

Using Technology

57   Check the final product

A presentation that looks great on your desktop computer often does not look as appealing when projected. Best to test it out on the actual equipment you will be using.

58   Preventing computer lockup

There can be many reasons for a computer locking up during a presentation. Try these preventative tips: 1) make sure you have enough memory, especially if you are using complicated graphics; 2) close out any applications not needed for the presentation; 3) consider lowering your screen resolution so graphics will refresh more quickly; 4) make sure you are using the same hardware and software that was successful in multiple dry runs.

Using Technology

59 Backup systems

Using technology has its risks. It's a good idea to take backup copies of any CD's you might be using as well as a backup CD for any software needed for the presentation. A zip drive can also be a useful backup tool. Make your presentation as failure proof as possible.

60 Low-tech insurance

Do you have a really high tech presentation with even higher stakes attached to the outcome? Consider hiring an IT technician to be your "caddy" and give you peace of mind that the technical side of things will be handled.

Using Technology

61   Send it ahead

Consider sending your presentation files ahead to the meeting site. Communicate with a technician on-site to make sure everything is loaded on the computer you will be using and running properly. And then take a back-up copy!

62   Using Web pages

It is very risky to use live web interaction during a presentation. It is better to embed screen captures into your slide show. You can simulate web interaction by moving rapidly from slide to slide.

Using Technology

63   Remote mouse

A great tool to use is a "remote mouse." This enables you to advance slides on your laptop from anywhere in the room and gives you more freedom to interact with the audience. In lieu of a remote mouse, a mouse with a long umbilical cord will at least give you some freedom of movement.

64   Video mute

Many LCD projectors have a "video mute" control that allows you to turn off the projected image using a remote control. This is a great tool to use when you want to direct attention to yourself, facilitate a discussion, or minimize the distraction of a slide showing on the screen.

Using Technology

65   Function F7

Most laptops have a function-F7 command that will
turn off the projected image from your laptop (the
"F" key may differ on some models). See "video
mute" above for the benefits of this tool.

66   Laser pointers

I personally dislike laser pointers and I have found
that most people find them distracting. If you insist
on using a laser pointer, avoid using it like a light
saber (ala Luke Skywalker) and simply use the light
to quickly direct the audience's attention to a specific location on your slide.

Using Technology

67   How to avoid using a laser pointer

The need to use a laser pointer typically indicates
that your slides are too busy. Consider re-designing
the slide to make better use of selective color to
highlight locations on the slide or use presentation
software capabilities to circle, build, or otherwise
highlight key points.

68   Microphones

Microphones almost always cause some problems.
Practice using a mike prior to a presentation. The
easiest microphone to use is the lavaliere (lapel) mike
that attaches to your clothing. Make sure you dress
properly to allow the mike to easily attach and have
a pocket for the transmitter (an especially important
consideration for women).

Using Technology

69 Using video

You can incorporate video using a standard VCR or with a laptop. If you are using a VCR, make sure the video segment is cued up in a way that minimizes the number of buttons you need to push to make it play. Short digital video clips are very effective when run through your laptop. Be sure your hardware and software are configured properly to run the video flawlessly.

70 Video using a laptop

Make sure you have the right computer, the right format, and the right audio capability to make the video effective. Preferably, use the same equipment during your presentation that you used in your practice session.

Using Technology

71   Building graphics

One advantage of computer-based presentations is that you can "build" content in order to maintain the audience's focus on a specific component of your slide. Be selective in using this feature. If you have a simple word slide, it can be distracting to build each line. Building is best when you are going to spend a minute or two on each segment built on the slide.

72   Be selective with transitions

Presentation software allows you to use fancy transitions between slides. If you insist on using transitions such as a wipe, dissolve, or fly-in, pick one transition and stick with it. It is annoying when a speaker tries to use every transition available in a single presentation.

Using Technology

73   Don't overdo the bells and whistles

Presentation software packages allow you to animate your slides, have transitions between slides, and even add sound each time you add information. Be very selective in using these tools. Audiences are more interested in what you say than in your software skill.

Visual Aids

Visual Aids

74 Essential criteria

Every visual aid must meet the following criteria: 1) it must be necessary (necessity); 2) it must be the best way to show a concept (clarity); 3) it must be simple (simplicity); and 4) it must be visible (visibility). Make sure each of your visual aids meet these criteria.

75 When to use them

Always ask, "will a visual aid enhance the audience's understanding of what I am saying? If the answer is yes, use a visual aid. There is no valid rule that will tell you how many visual aids you need for a presentation. Just focus on the needs of the audience and you will end up with the right amount.

Visual Aids

76   Create your visual aids last

Speakers are tempted to jump on their computer and begin creating visual aids as soon as they are asked to give a presentation. But the creation of visual aids should be the last step in creating a presentation. Start creating visuals only after you have a defined purpose, a thorough understanding of the audience, and fully developed content. Remember, visual aids are only a tool—content is most important!

Visual Aids

77 Storyboarding

Use storyboarding in drafting visual aids. A storyboard is simply a visual representation of your presentation outline. Sketch a visual to match any main ideas or concepts in your presentation. Create a visual story to match your verbal content. It will save lots of time in designing your final visual aids.

78 Keep it simple

Text slides are the most commonly used visual aid by most business professionals. Keep them simple. Try to have no more than five lines per slide and 5 words per line. This is a guideline, not a rule, but strive for simplicity.

Visual Aids

79   Simple charts and graphs

The 5/5 guideline can also be applied to charts and graphs. Try to limit the number of bars on a bar chart to 5, and the number of lines on a graph to 5. This may not always be feasible, but try to keep charts and graphs as simple as possible.

80   10 seconds or less

A good visual aid should be understandable by an audience in 10 seconds or less, without the speaker saying a word.

Visual Aids

81   Be selective with color

Color can help you focus attention on one element of your slide. Try to minimize the use of color so that it does not detract from your key points. Two to three colors per slide is usually sufficient.

82   Choosing type style

It is best to use "san serif" type styles for any visual aid. Examples of sans serif fonts are Arial, Helvetica, Geneva, Tahoma, and Avant Garde. These type styles are "blocky" and project better using an LCD projector or an overhead projector.

Visual Aids

83   Type size

Use the largest type sizes you can to insure visibility. If possible, avoid any size less than 24 point.

84   Use icons instead of bullets

A simple way to improve a bulleted word slide is to use symbolic icons instead of the boring bullets. Choose icons that can enhance the theme of your presentation.

85   Color contrast

A dark background with light text is best for computer projection and 35 mm slides. A light background and dark text is best for overhead transparencies. Color contrast is the key to visibility.

Visual Aids

86   Be careful with red

Red is not clearly visible against the dark background preferred for computer-projected slides, yet many try to use this color for emphasis. Also, it's not a great idea to use red when discussing financial data.

87   The six-foot test of visibility

If you are using overhead transparencies, lay them on the floor and make sure they are easily read from a standing position. If you are using a laptop, stand back six feet and test for readability.

Visual Aids

88 Handouts

Handouts are visual aids. Handouts can be used for two purposes: 1) to help the audience follow your presentation; 2) to provide supplementary information or more detail about your presentation content. If your slides are properly designed, reproductions of three slides per page with space for notes is a great handout. Pass it out before you begin your presentation.

89 Use a professional

You are the content expert, not the graphic designer. If you need a truly professional, high-tech presentation, plan ahead and hire a professional designer to polish the look of your graphics. You need to spend most of your time on the content, not the look.

Visual Aids

90   Supplemental handouts

A handout that provides supplementary information or additional details is best handed out AFTER your presentation. Avoid giving your audience the temptation to read while you present. Refer to the availability of an additional handout that you will provide after the presentation.

Using Your Eyes

Using Your Eyes

91   How much is enough?

Effective eye contact is making a 2-second connection with a specific listener. One thousand one, one thousand two...that is enough. I have experimented with different intervals in many workshops and the consensus is that 2-second contact is perfect.

92   Get a response

Another way to gauge effective eye contact is to make contact with an individual until you get a non-verbal response—a nod, smile, or blinking of the eyes. Look for a signal that you have "connected" and then move on.

Using Your Eyes

93   Avoiding the eyes

Some speakers have trouble making direct eye
contact; they say it makes them lose their train of
thought. Even in small groups you can avoid direct
contact and still give the impression of being confident and in control. Just look at the bridge of the
nose or the forehead instead of the eyes; they won't
be able to tell the difference even at close range.

94   Why make eye contact?

In Western cultures, eye contact denotes confidence,
credibility, and comfort with your subject. It is a
powerful non-verbal that should be mastered by all
speakers.

Using Your Eyes

95 Don't forget the corners

Many speakers tend to make most of their eye contact in the middle of the room and forget about people who sit to the extreme right or left. Be expansive with your eye contact and draw in the complete room, don't forget the people in the corners.

96 The eye contact magnets

It doesn't matter how large the audience, speakers are drawn to the smiling faces and those who tend to show agreement with their talk through non-verbal gestures. Be aware of those who you are spending too much time making contact, don't forget the rest of the audience.

Using Your Eyes

97 Eye contact and Q&A

A common mistake during the Q-and-A session is the speaker devoting all of their eye contact to the person who asked the question. Remember, you still have an audience that needs to be involved in your response with both your verbal and non-verbal skills. Avoid the one-to-one dialogue during the Q-and-A session.

98 Eye contact in large groups—the zonal approach

You can give the impression that you are making personal eye contact even with groups of 100 or more. Divide the audience into 6-8 zones and identify a friendly face in each zone. Then, make intermittent eye contact with the person in each zone as you give your presentation.

Using Your Eyes

99   Eye contact in large groups—the patterned approach

Another approach is to follow a pattern when making eye contact in large groups. Follow a pattern that would look like a flattened infinity sign...move diagonally across the middle of the room from left to right, come up the right side, back across the room diagonally from right to left, up the left side...and slowly repeat.

100   Eye contact for emphasis

You can extend your eye contact on a specific individual if you want to make a point. Keeping eye contact for over 2 seconds with one individual can grab their attention and help you drive home a statement.

Using Your Eyes

101 Be erratic with eye contact

In small groups, it's best to make "erratic" eye contact. Try not to establish a predicable pattern, it will help create some positive tension that will help you maintain interest in your presentation.

102 Try not to read

Audiences will tune out quickly if you lose eye contact while reading too long from a book or notes (see the section on notes and scripts on page 113).

Ideas?

Mind Over Mutter:
160 Practical Tips for Giving Great Presentations

Handling the Nerves

Handling the Nerves

103   **Get out of your head**

Much of the nervousness created by public speaking comes from a fear of failure. We are worried about ourselves, not the audience. It is that voice in our head telling us all the negative things. When the focus becomes more on the audience and their needs, it is easy to get comfortable and start enjoying the experience. So, get out of your head...and into your heart. It's not about you and what you know, it's more about the audience and what you are sharing.

104   **Be prepared**

The best way to minimize nervousness is to be thoroughly prepared for the presentation. Be prepared, be relaxed, and be effective!

Handling the Nerves

105   You are only human

Most people get nervous before speaking to a group, regardless of the size. Realize that the anxiety is normal! Mark Twain once said there are only two types of speakers, those that are nervous and those that are liars.

106   You don't look as nervous as you feel

I have observed thousands of business presentations over the years, both in presentation skills classes and in day-to-day business activities. Based on my observations, I have calculated that 99.9% of the time presenters do not *look* as nervous as they *feel*. So, don't be so overly concerned with that internal anxiety you feel. It is something you feel inside, but is typically not detectable outside.

Handling the Nerves

107 Self Talk

A great technique to minimize the nerves is to use self-talk. Every time that voice in your head starts to plant seeds of doubt, replace it with a positive self-talk statement. "I am a relaxed, confident speaker." Enter "self talk" at www.google.com for a bunch of resources.

108 Learn a relaxation technique

I learned how to do "progressive relaxation" years ago and this technique has never failed me. Enter "relaxation" on the Google™ search engine and you will be able to access plenty of available relaxation methods. Find one that works and use it!

Handling the Nerves

109   Exercise

I always exercise the night before a presentation. Take a walk, ride a bike, go to the gym...do something to "take the edge off" your anxiety.

110   Get a good night's sleep

No need to say more, this one is obvious.

111   Practice in the room

Practice always helps minimize anxiety. It's best if you can do a dry run in the room where you will be presenting. This helps you become familiar with the environment and also helps make any visualization techniques more powerful.

Handling the Nerves

112 Watch what you eat

I try to avoid spicy foods the night before speaking
and also eat a fairly bland breakfast on the day of
the presentation. When the stomach begins to
churn, I want to be sure I can keep it under control.
Pasta, oatmeal, toast, and even grits seem to be
good choices for my "pre-game" meals.

113 Curl your toes

The "fight or flight" feeling we get during a presentation can be difficult to control. A technique that
works for me—and has worked for others—is to
control the adrenalin rush by rapidly curling your
toes in your shoes. It gives you an outlet for the
energy and will not be noticed by an audience
(unless you are wearing open-toed shoes).

Handling the Nerves

114   Slow down

Slowing your speech can help you breath and also minimize the anxiety, especially when beginning your presentation. Try speaking a little slower at the outset of your talk until you gain some confidence and get in the flow.

Notes:

Mind Over Mutter:
160 Practical Tips for Giving Great Presentations

Tackling Questions

Tackling Questions

115   **Three guidelines for handling questions**

Just remember to be prepared, be brief, and be in control!

116   **Timing of questions**

The speaker can control when questions are asked by setting some ground rules. In your opening, state when you will allow questions: 1) after you have finished your presentation; 2) any time during the presentation; or 3) after main points in your presentation.

Tackling Questions

117 Restating the question

You only need to restate the question if the room is large and you want to insure that everyone has heard the question; or if it is a complicated question that requires you to restate and paraphrase to insure understanding.

118 Being prepared

A great way to anticipate questions is to conduct a practice presentation with some of your colleagues. Ask them to help you prepare for possible questions from the audience.

Tackling Questions

119 **Being brief**

Remember, you are answering a question, not beginning a new presentation. Keep your answers concise and focused on the question. Resist the potential urge to pontificate or expound on the topic—you risk generating more questions that may keep you from achieving the objective of your presentation.

Tackling Questions

120   Learn by observation

I have learned a lot about answering questions by watching White House, Pentagon, and State Department briefings. They are pros at staying on target and focused on a message. Tune into the news networks and learn from some skilled professionals.

121   Prompt questions

If you really want questions, prompt the questions by using a gesture. While asking, "Are there any questions?", walk toward the audience and raise your hand.

Tackling Questions

122   Use your non-verbal listening skills

When someone asks a question, demonstrate your interest by using non-verbal listening skills such as nodding, leaning towards them slightly, and making sincere eye contact.

123   When you don't have the answer

The worst thing you can do is give a wrong answer. It is best to defer, but don't apologize. Ask if you can get back with them with a thorough, accurate answer as soon as possible—and follow through on your promise!

Tackling Questions

124   Deferring to a colleague

If you don't have an answer, it may be appropriate to defer to a colleague who is prepared to answer the question. Plan ahead for this scenario by thoroughly anticipating the types of questions you may be asked. And be sure your colleague returns control of the meeting to you once they have answered.

125   Ground rules help with interruptions

If you have set ground rules in your opening as to when you will allow questions, you are in position to tactfully delay answering questions that result from interruptions. Simply restate the ground rule and ask if they can wait until the designated time.

Tackling Questions

126 Choose a strategy for answering

If you are interrupted by a question, you have three options: 1) go ahead and answer; 2) partially answer and defer a full answer until later; or 3) defer completely. If a question supports a point you are making, it may be best to answer it completely.

127 Know your key points

Knowing the key points and being comfortable with the flow of your presentation is essential for recovering from a question that interrupts your train of thought. Simply recap the main points, and redirect the listeners to the specific point you were addressing prior to the interruption.

Tackling Questions

128   Maintain your professionalism

Avoid confrontations with questioners if at all
possible. Keep cool; the audience will respect your
efforts to control your emotions.

129   Concentrate on what, not who

Very rarely are you challenged as an individual.
Rather, it is the content of your presentation that is
being questioned. Keep the discussion focused on
the content, not personalities.

Tackling Questions

130 Keep everyone involved

A common mistake made by many speakers is turning the Q-and-A session into a dialogue with a few people who are asking the questions. If your answer to a question requires more than two or three sentences, make sure to broaden your eye contact and engage the entire group as you would during your presentation.

Tackling Questions

131 Remember your VIP's

Every presentation has some VIP's—very important points. Use the Q-and-A session to bridge back to your points of emphasis. For example, you are asked the question, "Are you concerned about meeting next quarter's budget?" Your answer ties back to the fiscal controls that were emphasized in your presentation, "No, the cost accountability measures we have introduced will make budget management much easier."

132 What do you mean?

A technique for diffusing a hostile question is to ask, "What do you mean?" This forces the questioner to restate the question and gives you time to settle yourself and avoid making a terse response.

Tackling Questions

133 Descending levels of agreement

A questioner may be more interested in sharing their own viewpoint. If you agree with their point of view, go ahead and say so. Or you may agree with parts of their point of view, or how things could be as they suggest. Finally, you can agree on their right to having a differing viewpoint. Look for the win-win solution.

134 Offer to meet later

One way to diffuse a questioner who is belaboring a point and preventing you from proceeding with the rest of your presentation is to ask to meet them after the talk. If you request this diplomatically, they will usually comply.

Using Your Body

Using Your Body

135 The neutral position

A common question is "where do I put my hands?"
The best place to put your hands is in a neutral
position between your waist and your chest. Place
them lightly together, one on top of the other or in a
"steeple" configuration. From neutral, your movements will be more visible and have more meaning.

136 Smile, the forgotten gesture

One of the most powerful non-verbal gestures is the
smile. Yet many business presenters are so serious
that they forget about this simple tool. When
appropriate, use your smile to build rapport and
show enthusiasm about your topic.

Using Your Body

137 Congruence

Your verbal and non-verbal message needs to be congruent. If you can support a verbal with an effective non-verbal, your message will be even more powerful. If verbals and non-verbals do not agree, people tend to believe the non-verbal message.

138 Nervous habits

One of the best ways to identify nervous habits is to watch yourself on video. Habits such as rocking, swaying, tapping pointers, or using a repetitive gesture will become obvious, especially if you watch the tape in fast forward mode. Use video to minimize or eliminate bad habits.

Using Your Body

139 Hands in the pockets

There is no rule that says you can't put your hands in your pockets. It can be a very effective gesture that indicates you are relaxed and casual. Just be selective in its use, and be sure to empty your pockets of any objects before you speak (expecially coins and keys).

140 Stay square

It is best to stay "square" with the audience. Avoid turning your back, especially when pointing to information on a screen. Think of yourself as wearing a sweater with a number on the back. You don't want the audience to see the number.

Using Your Body

141 Building gestures

You can build a repertoire of effective gestures through practice. Review your presentation and look for ways to enhance your message with your body. Practice using a gesture when you rehearse and incorporate the movement into your presentation.

142 Slow motion

Gestures that are slow and sincere tend to have the greatest impact. Practice using slow motion gestures.

Using Your Body

143 Meaningful movement

Movement is a powerful tool for making transitions. A change in position while moving from one main point in your presentation to another will help signify a transition. The verbal message is supported by non-verbal movement.

144 Punctuate the point

Movement towards an audience can help you emphasize a key point. Come out from behind a lectern, move away from your laptop, and move closer to the listeners when emphasizing a point. It will provide an element of change and a non-verbal exclamation point.

Using Your Body

145 What to wear?

As a guideline, always be as well dressed as the best dressed person in the audience.

Ideas?

Mind Over Mutter:
160 Practical Tips for Giving Great Presentations

Videoconferencing

Videoconferencing

146 Limitations

Videoconferencing limits your body language and the rapport you can develop in a live presentation. Be aware that your voice becomes even more important in delivering a message. Use your vocal skills to have greater impact, speak very clearly and be sure to articulate your words.

147 Timing is important

Videoconferences often have time constraints. Make sure your presentation is focused and practice enough to have the timing fairly accurate.

Videoconferencing

148 Eye contact

Eye contact during a videoconference is focused on the remote site. If you have a live audience in addition to those at remotes sites, make occasional eye contact with the live group with the majority being on the remote site.

149 Visual aids and videoconferencing

Send copies of all of your visual aids and additional handout material to the remote site(s) ahead of time. Even if you are using document cameras or other graphic capabilities, audience members will find it easier to read your visuals using a handout.

Videoconferencing

150   Watch what you wear

Wear solid colors to a videoconference with colors in the pastel category being the best choice. Depending on the bandwidth available for the conference, stripes and patterns can become distracting because of their distortion when transmitted through video.

Notes & Scripts

Notes & Scripts

151   Notes are a great tool

There is no rule that says you cannot use notes in a business presentation. Notes can add to your confidence and help you stay focused. The key to using notes is to make them a constructive, not distracting, tool in the presentation.

152   Boiling it down to basics

One way to prepare a presentation is to write out your talk word for word. After reading your presentation a few times, create notes from the manuscript. Rehearse again using just the notes. And then consolidate the notes even further to a few key words.

Notes & Scripts

153 Practice with your final notes

Always practice with the final version of your notes so you are familiar with the location of key words or visual prompts.

154 5x7 Cards

A great way to use notes is to boil down your main points and supporting key words to three or four 5x7 cards. Simply arrange the cards on the table next to your laptop or overhead projector. Make the print large enough to see from a standing position, and refer to them as necessary.

Notes & Scripts

155 Flip charts

Flip charts still have a useful role in informal pre-sentations and small group settings. You can put your notes directly on a flip chart by lightly apply-ing in pencil. No one will notice your notes; it can even make you appear to be a great artist as you skillfully trace an existing pencil drawing during your presentation.

156 Software notes

Presentation software packages allow you to easily produce speaker notes. However, the default font for the notes is typically too small to read during a presentation. If you want to use this function, be sure to make the notes large enough and bold enough to read while you are presenting.

Notes & Scripts

157   Speaking from a script

There may be the rare occasion when you are required to read from a prepared script (public relations response, legal response, corporate policy statements). Presentations can be effectively delivered from a script but you need to practice the delivery even more than in an extemporaneous talk. The mistake many people make is feeling that because they will be reading prepared text, they do not need to practice.

158   Preparing a script

Use these guidelines when preparing a script: 1) double or triple space the text to make it easier to read; 2) always use upper and lower case letters; 3) number the pages; 4) only use the upper two-thirds of the paper for the text, this keeps you from having to look too far down.

Notes & Scripts

159 Choreograph the script

Insert reminders to yourself to emphasize keys words or phrases (underline, bold text), use slash marks in the text to remind yourself to slow down, and insert symbols as reminders to use a visual aid, refer to a document, or ask a question of the audience.

160 Number the pages

Always number the pages of your script or notes. You might drop them!

Submit a Tip

Many of the tips included in this book have come from friends, colleagues, and students who have attended my workshops over the years. Do you have a tip you would like to share in future editions of this book? Submit it to:

barry@pyramidresource.com

For more information about Barry Mitsch and The Pyramid Resource Group, Inc., visit:

www.pyramidresource.com

Notes:

Mind Over Mutter:
160 Practical Tips for Giving Great Presentations

Index

Mind Over Mutter:
160 Practical Tips for Giving Great Presentations

Mind Over Mutter:
160 Practical Tips for Giving Great Presentations